W9-BJF-033

Praise for *You Said What?*

"In spite of what you may believe, it is what you say and it is how you say it. The way you speak will determine your pathway to success. *You Said What?* is your guidebook."

–Jeffrey Gitomer
Author, *The Little Red Book of Selling*

"In today's business environment—where good customer service is now the price of entry—great, personalized service is the differentiator. Kim and Kerry help the reader understand the little things they can do to differentiate themselves in their marketplace."

—Todd Brown
Marketing manager, Cadillac Escalade and SRX

"Few people are born with a natural gift for communications; the rest of us would benefit greatly from taking this material to heart!"

—Geoffrey O'Connell
Partner, Accenture

"If you aren't where you should be in your career, it's an extremely good bet that the problem is how you communicate. I've seen every one of the mistakes Zoller and Preston describe (and I've made many myself), and any one of them can torpedo your success if not corrected. *You Said What?* is the most straightforward and practical guidebook to improving your communications I've ever read, and I'm recommending this book to every employee of mine who wants to achieve more in their professional lives."

—Doug Leeds
CEO, Ask.com

You Said
What?

You Said
What?

The Biggest Communication Mistakes
Professionals Make

Kim Zoller · Kerry Preston

Brown Books Publishing Group
Dallas, Texas

© 2012 Kim Zoller and Kerry Preston

All rights reserved. No part of this book may be used or reproduced in any manner without written permission except in the case of brief quotations embodied in critical articles or reviews.

You Said What?
The Biggest Communications Mistakes Professionals Make

Brown Books Publishing Group
16250 Knoll Trail Drive, Suite 205
Dallas, Texas 75248
www.BrownBooks.com
(972) 381-0009

A New Era in Publishing™

ISBN: 978-1-61254-060-3
Library of Congress Control Number 2012939171

Printing in the United States
10 9 8 7 6 5 4 3 2 1

For more information, please visit: www.IDImage.com

This book is dedicated to all of our clients
for supporting us through our journey.

Contents

Acknowledgments

We truly thank each other for an outstanding partnership of more than twelve years. We are lucky enough to have become the best of friends over that time. We help each other remember that we always have to continue to grow personally and we can always get better.

Many thanks to our wonderful clients and seminar participants for asking thought-provoking questions and for their active participation. This book was written with them and their colleagues in mind.

We want to acknowledge the work of Shawn Mash, Susan Klein, Paula Zeitman, and Harriet Whiting for their contributions and fascinating ideas about communication, and Lauren Feinstein and Adam Tobolowsky for their contributions to the chapter on social media.

We are incredibly grateful to our mothers, Harriet Whiting and Kathleen Preston.

We thank and acknowledge our husbands, Tim Reinagel and Keith Lebowitz, who gave us many hours to let us complete this book.

We thank our families, especially our children—Benjamin, Samuel, Luke, Wes, and Nate.

Introduction

"You can have brilliant ideas, but if you can't get them
across, your ideas won't get you anywhere."

—Lee Iacocca

Wouldn't it be nice if every time the person with whom
we are speaking heard us exactly the way in which we
intended? Why isn't that the case many times? Things get in the
way of our words. Have you ever said or heard someone say, "That
wasn't my intention"? Intention only means something when our
communication is presented in such a way that the other person's
perceptions correlate to what was intended. If they don't match,
you end up with, "You said *what*?"

Communication is *presence*. It is not about words or actions
separately but about how those words and actions together
translate into our overall message. Presence. It is the way we
present ourselves. It is how we build consistent credibility
through every mode of communication.

You Said What? is a holistic view of how we communicate
our message. Communication embodies many areas, and by
being holistic—looking at the big picture—we can ensure that
we are focusing on every way we present ourselves, not on just
one area. For example, communication style is a very important
and "hot" topic—as it should be. If we're just focused on adapting

to someone's style without taking into account what experiences they bring to the table, we may miss connecting with that person and ultimately may not reach our communication goal.

It is very easy to focus on one part of communication, such as the way we speak, yet this is a very small part of what this book discusses. Focusing on one small part of communication will never get the result we're looking for. Sociologist Albert Mehrabian says that our words account for only 7 percent of the impression we make.

We are constantly communicating. We may never speak a word, but we may have said a mouthful. In almost two decades of being in this business, we have seen countless talented and intelligent individuals lose opportunities because of the way they communicated their overall message. We have seen them fail because of the way they present themselves and the impressions they make, which correlate to their overall communication presence. On the flip side, we have also watched and followed people who "get it." They plan and they think about what they are doing and saying to make sure they are heard.

Communication is not how and what we say; it is *how we are heard*. It is not about us; it is about how the other person perceives our message and us.

Our goal for you while reading this book is that you take a step back, think about what you are really trying to accomplish, and build a plan around the way you communicate. From your words to your nonverbal communication to your brand, every single way in which you communicate can affect your outcome.

During our communication skills seminars over the last nineteen years, we have asked more than five thousand participants, "What are the barriers and challenges to good communication?" Here is a snapshot of their replies:

- Diversity
- Unclear direction
- Perception
- Language barriers
- Lack of knowledge
- Poor planning
- Lack of resources
- Poor listening skills
- Emotion
- Lack of approachability
- Anger
- Hidden or preconceived agendas
- Time constraints
- Preconceptions
- Ineffective verbal/written skills
- Body language
- Lack of organizational skills
- Overwhelming personality
- Intimidation
- Fear of vulnerability
- Lack of preparation
- Lack of information
- Lack of face time (shifts, geography, scheduling)
- Fear of change
- Lack of self-confidence
- Too many stakeholders
- No listening/all talk
- Fear of consequences
- Feeling that opinion matters
- Poor attitude
- Inarticulateness
- Lack of trust
- Too much jargon
- Disinterest in topic
- Inflexibility
- Different backgrounds/ cultures
- Message not being communicated down the chain of command
- Different work styles
- Bad public speaking skills
- Poor nonverbal skills
- Not knowing audience
- Distractions
- People (in general)
- Unfamiliarity with material
- Confusion about end goals
- Lack of passion
- Lack of inspiration

This book has been written based on the feedback we've received. *You Said What?* is an action-oriented book to help you reach your goal. Get your message across by planning and taking the time to sharpen your communication skills.

Big Mistake

1

Not Being on Your A-Game

"The door to success is sticking."

"Yesterday's home runs don't win today's games."
—Babe Ruth

What difference does one degree make? If you're hot when it's 95 degrees, you'll still be hot when it's 96 degrees. Water is extremely hot at 211 degrees, but at 212 degrees it boils. Boiling water creates steam, which is strong enough to power a train. That one degree changes the game. Imagine what it would take for you to change your game.

Thought and planning are the keys to making a difference in your communication style and approach. You have an opportunity either to make a difference or to be the same as everyone else. Is it worth it to think things through a little more? One degree more? Or is the status quo easier?

Being on your A-game is a mind-set. It's an overall positive attitude toward the differences you want to make in your own life and in others' lives. Think about it: If every time there was a conflict and you took a step back to be solution-driven, wouldn't you be a difference maker? Wouldn't it make life easier for you and for others around you?

You may recognize this scenario. The plane is delayed and someone—maybe you—is not going to make his or her connection. Not only is the flight delayed, but it is also overbooked and the passenger has lost his seat. He is yelling and screaming at the airline representative. The representative looks back and says with a short and rude tone, "There is nothing I can do. Please have a seat." The passenger is furious, and the fight is just beginning.

On the other hand, if either the passenger or the airline representative had been on their A-game, the situation would have had a completely different sound and feel. Interestingly enough, the outcome may not change, but the chances are about 80 percent that either the representative would want to help or the passenger would calm down because of a composed, empathetic, and professional conversation with the representative.

Having a positive attitude doesn't mean walking around with a big smile on your face all day every day. It means taking a breath when something goes wrong. It means looking at worst-case scenarios and thinking about the solution rather than focusing on the problem and who caused that problem. It means being open and present, not closed to what is going on around you. It also means knowing that you can't control everything. Ultimately it means controlling your reactions.

The bottom line is that people do not want to be around negative people. They don't want to work with people they cannot communicate with in a positive way.

According to a study conducted by the Carnegie Institute of Technology, 15 percent of the reason you get a job, keep a job, and move ahead in that job is determined by your technical skills and knowledge—regardless of your profession—and 85 percent is determined by your people skills and people knowledge, including your enthusiasm, smile, tone of voice, personal responsibility, and moral and ethical excellence.

The outcome of our communication is driven by our ability to get along.

There are best practices throughout this book—we challenge you to always use them. If you do, the outcome of your interactions will change. We've tested these practices ourselves, we've observed the communications of others, and we've interviewed thousands of people about what they believe are the keys to effective communication. When we handle things while being on our A-game, we always have a positive outcome.

Best Practices
- Monitor your tone.
- Try to understand where the other person is coming from.
- Listen to others.
- Be prepared.
- Set simple goals for your interactions with others.
- Focus on things that make a difference.
- Try to offer help to others.
- Stay calm.
- Plan out hypothetical worst-case scenarios.

Ask Yourself These Crucial Questions
- Have I seen an outcome turn from negative to positive based on the way I handled the situation?
- Am I affected by someone else's negative attitude? Have I communicated differently because of that negative attitude? How has that affected my A-game?

- Have I ever lost a job or a promotion when I thought my skills were a perfect fit? What am I not seeing?

Take the time to think about the outcome you are trying to achieve and always be on your A-game by following best practices.

Big Mistake

2

Not Beginning with the End in Mind

"All that we are is the result of
what we have thought."
—Buddha

Think before you speak. This is such a basic concept, yet it is so hard to put into practice. Everything we say has a consequence—positive or negative. If we don't know our big-picture goal, our communication can affect the outcome in a negative way. If we know our goal and we think through the "why," "what," and "how," we have a better chance of impacting our relationships in a positive way. There are spontaneous conversations, and there are conversations for which we have time to plan and think while keeping the end goal in mind.

--------- On the Side ---------

"A colleague of mine recently said he was upset that I didn't include him in a meeting he thought he should have been invited to. This was a spontaneous conversation where someone was upset with me, and I didn't have an opportunity to plan my response. I could have reacted and responded in many different ways. Engaging in a negative way could have created other problems. This situation made me realize I need to be mindful of the words I use to achieve my goals."

—Social media manager for an events company

If someone does something that you don't like or agree with, do you tell them? Well, what's your goal? Do you know what actually happened, or are you making assumptions about what happened? If you say something, what will the outcome look like? Is there a potential to create problems and break down a long-term relationship because of a judgment or feeling you have? Be aware that some bridges can never be rebuilt.

Best Practices

- Realize that the past can affect someone's perception about a situation.
- When possible, plan your conversation to make sure your communication matches your goal.
- Think about your timing and its effects; the context of a situation can affect everything.
- Everyone has their own agenda; look at both sides.
- Seek clarity before making assumptions.
- Think before you speak. Even when you are put on the defensive, remember your goal.
- Think about what you will achieve by saying something.

Ask Yourself These Crucial Questions

- Have I ever wished that I could take back something I said to a colleague?

- If I could change the outcome, what would I do differently the next time? What did I learn?
- How can I better manage my reactions and emotions to reach my communication and relationship goals?

Big Mistake

3

Not Knowing Your Personal Brand

"Regardless of age, regardless of position, regardless of the business we happen to be in, all of us need to understand the importance of branding. We are CEOs of our own companies: Me, Inc. To be in business today, our most important job is to be head marketer for the brand called You."

—Tom Peters

How do personal branding and communication go together? Everything you say—verbally and nonverbally—is your brand. If you don't think you have a brand, you're wrong. You do. Others come to expect you to communicate a certain way based on their past experience with you. How you send e-mails, when you text, how you deal with problems, how you give compliments, how you take criticism . . . the list does not end.

In the previous chapter, we explored your goal. Branding yourself is 100 percent tied into that goal and is a critical component of being heard.

Before we go further, think about the goal you have in mind. Which of your behaviors support that goal? Are you consistent? You build your brand through consistently communicating what people can expect from you. Build and market your brand rather than letting others decide it for you.

We must invest in our brands. Everything from how we look to what we learn, how we grow, our personal and professional development—all of these are components of our investment. These are all areas for you to invest in to protect your brand.

Go into the lobby of any hotel or place of business and observe the surroundings. You can immediately describe that entity's brand. Your dress is your brand's decor. People notice and can describe you, yet you haven't said a word.

Because we work in a very image-driven business world, we notice how much attention successful individuals apply to their brand. It is attention to detail and consistency, and it requires forethought and taking that extra step to make sure that all of your communications send the same message.

On the Side

"I was conducting a seminar for a large manufacturing company, and one of the executives told me a story of how he had once said to his boss that he liked what he was doing and didn't want to be a manager. His boss branded him, and while he worked for her, he was never promoted. He now realizes how he built that brand and wasn't able to readjust until he changed departments."

— Kim Zoller

Best Practices

- Behavior needs to be consistent in order to build a brand that people come to respect.
- Your brand has to be adaptable to your environment and situation but authentic to yourself.
- Opt for quality rather than quantity with wardrobe selection.
- Dress your brand every day; it makes a difference.
- Don't forget that even details like e-mails support or detract from your brand.
- Select words that build your brand and stay away from slang.
- Stay away from negative chitchat; you can destroy your brand through negative talk and gossip.
- Game on! Put your best foot forward.

Ask Yourself These Crucial Questions

- Do all of my communications support my personal brand? Am I living my brand every day through every interaction?
- Do I have a mentor or someone I respect in business? What is their brand? How is their communication consistent?
- How can I tie in my daily interactions and tasks with my personal brand initiative?

Big Mistake

4

Not Managing Perceptions

"There are things known and there are things unknown, and in between are the doors of perception."
—Aldous Huxley

Perceptions affect the outcome of our communication. The way we walk, the way we hold ourselves, the way we dress, how we carry our briefcase, the look of the briefcase, our smile or lack of one—the list could go on. The impression we make on other people many times determines how well they communicate with us. Bad first impressions generally lead to bad relationships. Good first impressions give us the opportunity to build rapport and establish good two-way communication.

What makes perception reality is that we are dealing not only with our communication efforts but also with the experiences of the receiver of the communication.

In 1955 the Johari Window, a cognitive pyschological tool, was created by sociologists Harry Ingham and Joseph Luft. The Johari Window is used to help people better understand their interpersonal communication and relationships. It gives us an understanding of how people may hear things differently from how we intended, and it also helps us look at our own self-awareness and how that self-awareness affects our overall communication.

With this understanding, if we have good and open communication with people, we can solicit feedback to help us understand how we are heard and perceived.

Johari Window		
	Things You Know About You	Things You Don't Know About You
Things Others Know	Public Knowledge Open/Free Area	Blind Spot Blind Area
Things Others Don't Know	Secret Unknown Area	Unknown Potential Unknown Area
Reprinted from Joseph Luft and Henry Ingham, "The Johari window, a graphic model of interpersonal awareness."		

To understand the Johari Window, it is important to recognize that:
- Public Knowledge/Open/Free Area represents what we know about ourselves and what others know about us.
- Blind Spot/Blind Area represents what others notice about us that we do not realize.
- Secret/Unknown Area represents things that we have not and do not want to share with others.
- Unknown Potential/Unknown Area represents what we do not know about ourselves and what others do not know either. This area is generally explored in therapy.

──────────── **On the Side** ────────────

This was told to us by one of our clients after she learned about the Johari Window:

"One day a woman I've known for a long time called me. She is the mother of a child at the school my kids attend. She has never said a word to me. She hardly even looks at me when I pass her in the parking lot or the school hallway. We have been at many of the same functions and parties, and she has never smiled or spoken to me—just completely ignored me. In fact, every time someone introduces us, she looks at me as though she has not met me at least ten times before.

"I have always been totally put off by her and have always thought she was rude. So when my phone rang and it was her, I was extremely surprised that she even knew my name. She asked if she could come in to discuss something with me and I said, 'Yes.' I was curious to hear what she had to say. Well, she was looking for a job. The most interesting thing about the conversation was that she went on and on about how people always tell her that she should be in a position where she is around people. How great she is around people and that she has been told that she has the most endearing personality. I wanted to say to her, 'Are you sure they were talking about you?'"

—Leadership development director

───────────────────────────────────────

This woman was definitely in the Blind Spot of the Johari Window.

Self-perception can be a strange thing if there's no awareness, self-reflection, or feedback from people you trust. It's hard to have a good channel of communication when people perceive you differently from how you perceive yourself.

Best Practices

Dress

- Dress appropriately every day for every situation.
- Think before you wear something that may convey the wrong message.
- Do not risk losing respect just to be comfortable.
- Think about who you might meet or see and whether your attire represents your brand.

Body Language

Your body language speaks volumes about your feelings or others' perceptions of your feelings. Be aware of what you are communicating without even opening your mouth.

- Keep your shoulders back and your head up.
- Have a firm and appropriate handshake.
- Hold eye contact when shaking someone's hand.
- Make eye contact and do not look around when engaged in conversation.
- Smile when appropriate.
- Do not fidget with your hair, pen, change in your pocket, or anything else that will distract from what you are saying.

Conversation

- Stay positive; do not talk about negative things.
- Maintain a good attitude.
- Be prepared.

- Stay focused—be present.
- Be concise; do not chatter.
- Be interested, not interesting.

In Meetings
- Verbal and nonverbal communication speak loudly in meetings.
- Speak up and be present.
- Speak with confidence when you have something to add, not just to talk.
- Introduce yourself. You are your brand.

Body Language That Gets in Your Way
- Walking around with a serious look all the time—people assume you have too much on your plate and that you are not approachable.
  - » **Solution:** smile.
- Being disorganized and harried all the time—people assume you cannot handle your work.
  - » **Solution:** clean your desk, slow down, look up, breathe.
- Be aware of:
  - » Sounds of verbal frustration, e.g., "tsk"
  - » Heavy sighs
  - » Crossed arms
  - » Eye rolling and eye fluttering
  - » Looking down
  - » Head shaking

Ask Yourself These Crucial Questions

- What are the five words other people use to describe me?
- Am I perceived the way I want to be perceived? If there is a gap, what actions can I take to close that gap?
- How do I become more self-aware? What type of feedback do I need to search out from someone I trust?

Big Mistake

5

Not Connecting and Building Relationships

"I know I wronged you on the way up,
but I'm much nicer now that I'm here."

"The most important single ingredient in the formula of
success is knowing how to get along with people."
—Theodore Roosevelt

This chapter addresses two topics: the personal and emotional
connections we make with others and how we network to
build connections. These topics are tied together very closely.

Companies spend billions of dollars on marketing and public
relations in order to build trust and likeability of their brand or
product. Similarly, millions of people go to networking groups
to establish connections that build trust and likeability so that
they can do business or be referred. We create value by building
connections, and we build value in ourselves by connecting with
other people on a personal level.

Are you connecting with those around you? Communication
is about the connections we make with others and how they then
communicate about you to others. Connecting is very important:
just look at the success of LinkedIn or any of the other social
media websites that help make connecting easier.

On the Side

"Recently I walked into a jewelry store and saw something I loved. I didn't know the store or the owner, who was helping other customers. The store looked busy and people seemed to be buying, so I thought it was probably a reputable place, but I wanted to make sure. I pulled out my phone and used Google to check reviews about the store. Within minutes I found a bad review from the Better Business Bureau. I walked right out. Keep in mind that that review could have been the result of just one person's complaint. It's unfortunate, but it speaks to how closely we are all connected."

—Real estate agent

We build trust by doing great work. We also build trust by being recommended by our network. It is always better for someone else to tell someone how great we are than to tell that person ourselves. They will believe it far more when it comes from another source. As you work toward your goals, keep in mind how everyone is interconnected. When you build bridges, it is easier to get to a person through someone who already knows and trusts you.

Best Practices
Building Bridges
Are you building bridges? If something negative has happened with someone, remember that they have a network too and that we are all separated from one another by only a few degrees.

- Apologize if you have done something that another person has perceived negatively.
- Do what you can to remedy the situation.

- Do not go over anyone's head to get to another person unless you have thought through the situation and you know the outcome will be what you want.
- Do not go over someone's head just to get immediate results, as this may burn a bridge.
- If you do go over someone's head, be aware that you may burn one bridge to build another.
- Be inclusive; it helps build bridges.
- When working on a project, make sure you are including everyone involved in e-mails, calls, etc.

Networking

Are you using your channels to network and communicate your message?

- Keep in touch with people you meet.
- Follow up with a phone call or a note when you have made a good connection.
- Don't follow up with someone only when you need something.
- Introduce people to other people who can help them achieve their goals.
- Don't be afraid to ask someone to refer you to someone else if you have a good relationship.
- Prove yourself through top-notch work before you ask someone to do anything for you.
- Be there when people need you.

Elevator Speech

Can you explain who you are in ninety-nine seconds or less? It's hard to come up with an elevator speech if you don't know your brand. There are two types of elevator speeches: one for telling someone what you do and another for when someone asks you how you are and what you've been doing lately. You have to prepare and practice both and realize that your elevator speeches can determine the longevity of the conversation.

The key elements of your elevator speech are:
- Your full name
- Your position
- Something interesting you do that is quickly explained and easy to understand
- Your aspirations

Keep in mind that you need to tailor your elevator speech to your audience. For example, talking to an external customer is different from talking to a key decision maker in your company.

Answering "What do you do?"
- Be brief and be clear.
- Try to relate what you do to something the person with whom you are speaking knows about. For example, ask a question to see if he or she is familiar with the type of work you do.
- Examples:
  - » "Have you ever been to a training workshop on building your communication skills? That's what I do."
  - » "I have a corporate training company where we do everything from writing a business process, to training that process, to writing and developing corporate universities to training personal and professional development skills like communication."

> » "I am the HR director for Big Star, and I handle all the employee benefits and recruiting."

Answering "How are you? What have you been doing lately?"

- Always be positive; no one wants to hear bad news.
- Thank the person for asking: "Thank you for asking . . ."
- Don't forget to ask them back, "How are you?"
- It's all right to repeat the question to buy time to respond: "What have I been up to? That's a good question . . ."
- Be ready to discuss some exciting things going on at work that do not sound like bragging.
- Examples:
  - » "I am doing well, thanks. Business has been really fun lately; I have been working on two big projects."
  - » "I am great, thanks. Luckily we're very busy and I have been meeting with some new clients and finding out their needs. I love that part of my job."

General Best Practices

- If you are meeting someone for the first time, stand up, shake their hand, make eye contact, smile, and introduce yourself with your full name, company, and position.
- Notice eye color; this helps you maintain eye contact.
- Stay positive.
- If they don't introduce themselves back, simply ask with a smile on your face, "What's your name? Where do you work?"
- Be prepared with questions to ask others.

- In any corporate environment, be able to identify the key executives.

Establishing Your BLT

Establishing believability, likeability, and trust is crucial to communicating our overall message. How do we do that?

- Be positive in all situations and stay on your A-game.
- Say only positive things about other people. If you say negative things about someone else, the person will automatically assume that you will say negative things about them too.
- Do not speak badly about your competitors.
- Do what you say you are going to do every time.
- Follow up in a timely manner.
- Apologize when you do not follow through or follow up when you said you would.
- Be interested in others, not interesting.

Ask Yourself These Crucial Questions

- Is there a bridge that I have burned that I need to rebuild? If yes, what is my timeline and action plan to rebuild it?
- What am I going to do from this point forward to ensure I do not burn a bridge?
- What techniques am I using to keep in touch and build my network? If I don't have any, what can I do to change that? Have I written notes to people who have helped me through the years? Is it time to start?

Big Mistake

6

Not Making Appropriate Small Talk

MY NEW YEAR'S RESOLUTION IS TO STOP PUTTING MY FOOT IN MY MOUTH ALL THE TIME... I'LL BET YOURS IS LOSING WEIGHT, HUH?...

Copyright ©2005 Creators Syndicate, Inc.

"Talk low, talk slow, and don't talk too much."

—John Wayne

How many times have you been in a situation where you couldn't believe what someone was saying to you? There are too many times when people make assumptions about others and offend without realizing that they're doing so. Building rapport in business does not mean telling everyone your personal information.

Do your research. Know who you're talking to, and be careful if you don't. Be prepared with topics to discuss so that you can engage in a meaningful conversation. We all know people love to talk about themselves. Ask "how," "what," and "why" questions to learn more about the other person and keep the conversation going. Clearly, rapport is not about "putting someone on the stand." It is more like a tennis match, going back and forth. It is about being genuine and authentic and realizing that finding common ground builds long-term relationships.

Good Questions to Ask

- "How did you get involved . . ."
- "Tell me more about . . ."
- "What are some of the challenges you face . . ."
- "What do you enjoy most about . . ."
- "When did you start . . ."
- "How did you prepare for . . ."
- "What's next for you . . ."

Topics to Discuss

- Career background
- Achievements and goals
- Hobbies and leisure activities
- Community involvement
- Entertainment (favorite movies and books)
- Current events (as long as they are not controversial)
- Family (as long as the other person brings it up first; do not get too personal)

Remember that just because you are a good talker does not mean that you are a good *small* talker. It takes practice and a willingness to learn about and enjoy other people. Let go of the anxiety of what you have to say and become interested in others. It is amazing how important a person feels when someone is interested in them.

———————————— On the Side ————————————

"I was incredibly close with one of my coworkers, Maxine. We really told each other everything, personal and professional. Last year Maxine was promoted, and everything seems to have changed. I regret telling her a lot of the things I told her. I feel that I am not being promoted because she thinks that I do not have a stable home life. I'm not sure what to do about it, but I have definitely learned to keep my personal life personal."

—Employee of an insurance company

Best Practices
Avoid getting into discussions on:
- Politics
- Religion
- Sexism
- Racist or ethnic comments
- Sexual orientation
- Salary
- Gossip
- Negativism
- Private matters
- Private family matters

Also Avoid
- Giving too much personal information
- Giving an overabundance of detail
- Interrogating rather than conversing
- Interrupting the other person
- Complaining
- Trying to "one-up" the other person
- Glancing around the room while someone is conversing with you

(You can find additional tips for making small talk in *You Did What? The Biggest Mistakes Professionals Make.*)

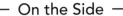

On the Side

"One of my biggest pet peeves is when a vendor shares their personal lives with me. I have too much to do and not enough time, and it is a waste of my time. I think there should be a book for salespeople and vendors titled *Know When to Stop Talking*! Now I just tell those specific vendors that I have exactly five minutes. I enjoy getting to know people, but some people just take it too far."

—Purchasing manager of a major airline

Ask Yourself These Crucial Questions

- If someone were telling me the same thing I'm telling them, would I think it was appropriate?
- Is this person really interested in what I am saying?
- Am I going to regret saying this at a later date?

Big Mistake

7

Meltdown of Communication through Technology Use

"I can't talk. I'm in an email mood."

"E-mail is a unique communication vehicle for a lot of reasons. However, e-mail is not a substitute for direct interaction."

—Bill Gates

All of us have been the victims of miscommunication through technological outlets. Simply put, one of the largest causes of this problem comes from the fact that it is close to impossible to convey in an e-mail or text the same tone, attitude, and manner that vocal inflections and facial expressions can communicate.

E-mail

E-mail is one of the largest causes of communication breakdowns. It is fast, easy, and gets our message out there, but it does not take into account the emotions that can be read into the message. Building rapport is the ultimate goal of communication, and an e-mail can ruin that rapport with the click of a mouse.

Daniel Goleman, author of numerous books, including *Emotional Intelligence*, says:

Reviewing studies on e-mail in the workplace from the new field of cyberpsychology . . . Kristin Byron at Syracuse University's business school finds that, in general, e-mailing ups the likelihood of conflict and miscommunication. One reason: we tend to misinterpret positive e-mail messages as more neutral, and neutral ones as more negative, than the sender intended. Even jokes are rated as less funny by recipients than by senders.

On the Side

"Recently I was in a negotiation to sell my company for a substantial amount of money. The prospective buyer asked me to e-mail my expectations for the buyout. I proceeded to be as direct as I could and wrote down everything I expected. After reading the e-mail a couple of times, I sent it. I then called the prospective buyer after sending the e-mail, and they were furious. They had read many additional messages into my e-mail that I thought were harmless. Needless to say, the deal didn't go through."

—Owner of a privately-owned printing company

Other factors that can harm overall communication when e-mailing are how an e-mail looks, how formal or informal it is, and whether it contains spelling errors. A typo or a misplaced word can cause the reader to question the professionalism of the sender. E-mail is a wonderful mode of communication when used in the correct way for the correct purpose. When you are trying to build or strengthen a relationship, pick up the telephone or walk to the other person's office instead. This will ensure that they are receiving the intended message.

─────────────── On the Side ───────────────

"An e-mail came and there were three typos. I could tell that it was sent quickly and in response to a question. Unfortunately the e-mail had been forwarded to two internal colleagues and external customers. When I was with one of the external customers, they made a comment to me about the e-mail, saying, 'Do you think that Dave is the right person for this project?' When I asked why they would say that, the customer mentioned the typos in the e-mail and stressed that the details were what made his company successful."

—Director of a PR firm

Best Practices

Format of the E-mail:

- Write an e-mail like a letter with a greeting, body, and closing.
- Do not use color or design as a background for a professional e-mail.
- Use punctuation correctly.
- Reread the e-mail slowly to ensure that there are no errors.
- Remember that spell check does not catch incorrect word usage, just misspelled words that do not exist.
- Be direct and to the point.

Send an E-mail:
- When you are relaying information with no emotional attachment.
- When you need to give a concise response.
- With less frequency than physical or telephone contact; make sure more direct contact is used with a 3:1 ratio to e-mail.
- If you would like to state a disclaimer by placing a phrase like "sensitive" or "do not forward" in the subject line.

Don't Send an E-mail:
- If the topic is emotional. Pick up the telephone or make an appointment to resolve the issue.
- If the other person becomes emotional during the e-mail exchange; pick up the telephone.
- If the e-mail exchange is going back and forth with no resolution; pick up the telephone and bring closure to the conversation.
- If the e-mail sounds the least bit emotional; if you are not sure, have someone objective read it.
- When you are angry or upset; do not ever put your feelings in writing.
- To your entire address book; send an e-mail only to the necessary parties.
- If it is a direct and lengthy response to only one person.
- If you risk projecting an image to your superiors that your day is spent mostly sending and reading e-mail and making them wonder what else you should be doing.
- If you do not wish to have it forwarded to others. If you place a disclaimer not to do so at the end of the e-mail,

be aware people often glance at e-mails and don't read all the way to the end.

(For additional tips on e-mail protocol, see *You Did What? The Biggest Mistakes Professionals Make.*)

Ask Yourself These Crucial Questions

- What message am I trying to send?
- Have I reread this e-mail enough times to catch any errors?
- Should I call or make an appointment with the person instead?

Texting

Texting can lead to all kinds of social faux pas. Keep these tips in mind:

- The biggest offense is texting while having a face-to-face conversation.
- Focus on the person in front of you.
- Just because your colleagues are texting doesn't mean that it is professional; look for ways to set yourself apart.
- Know when it is appropriate to use shorthand and emoticons.
- Texting should be your last alternative when communicating with a customer.
- Take the customer's lead with texting but realize that it doesn't ever take the place of a real conversation.

Ask Yourself These Crucial Questions
- What message am I trying to send?
- Does this message match my professionalism? Is it too casual?
- Should I call the person instead?

Big Mistake

8

Not Managing Your Social Networking

"Right, like the boss will know I'm
spending all day schmoozing on Facebook."

"Don't say anything online that you wouldn't want plastered on a billboard with your face on it."

—Erin Bury

——————————— On the Side ———————————

"Our recruiting team checks Facebook and other social media outlets for applicants. People are out of control with what they post. I recommend people ask themselves if they ever plan on being in business; if the answer is yes, then stay away. There is a reason that FBI agents and most law enforcement officials don't use Facebook personally—it can put too much in the open that people with bad intentions can use. The same goes for work."

—Partner of a consulting firm

Social media is an extension of your brand. Be smart, realize that nothing is private, and know that what you post can be used in a court of law. On the flip side, if social media is used well it can be a great way to make connections with business associates.

Keep in mind that everything you put online will be there forever. This can have implications for your professional life, no matter your age when you posted something or how long ago you posted it. Again, when something is posted online, it is there forever.

We have enlisted the expertise of social media gurus Lauren Feinstein and Adam Tobolowsky of Marketing Influence to contribute their best business-savvy advice for integrating social media into your business plan. This chapter is a joint effort from our side, focusing on building your "personal and professional brand," and their side, focusing on the specifics of social media. Here's what they have to say.

Many are apprehensive when approaching social media. They fear diving into something they possibly could not sustain. The importance of social media can be based only on how much work the user puts into it. Imagine an individual consumer seeking a specific product using only social media. That person would use search terms specific to his or her needs and choose the most credible looking account to make his or her purchase. A social media account that has been built but not maintained will more times than not get dropped for something more up-to-date. The viral nature of social media is undeniable and has recently been responsible for worldwide uprisings and changing of political regimes, yet people are still timid when using it to market their business. The power of social media is vast, and with the correct tools, *you can succeed!*

LinkedIn

- LinkedIn is a virtual résumé and networking site that is strictly for business use.
- LinkedIn is a professional/social networking site as opposed to a social/social networking site.
- LinkedIn is a tool for the entry-level employee all the way up the line to the CEO.
- On the ground level, sourcing is made easier for those account managers seeking a decision maker. On the other end, a CEO can manage his expansive list of contacts as well as present a demonstrative leadership persona to others.

Best Practices

- Keep your updates business related.
- Your professional credibility can be put at stake by any questionable or politically incorrect postings.
- Postings should be less frequent, putting more emphasis on professional quality rather than quantity.
- Groups can be used to expand your personal and professional brand. Joining groups and exposing yourself to new potential contacts that have the same professional interest as you will enable you to present your thoughts to unique eyes.
- An insightful comment can go a long way. This is an important tool for any professional making new connections through current connections.
- Make sure your page is well-written and well-thought-out.
- Proofread for errors, keep your information clear, and be concise (people want the bottom line).

By using the tools LinkedIn provides, you will be able to efficiently connect, organize, and even reconnect with past, current, and future networks. For example, when asked to specify "How Do You Know This Person," fill content diligently so as to categorize and retain contacts over years of experience. When the time comes, you will be prepared.

On the Side

"I can't believe how many college students put inappropriate photos of themselves online. Do they not realize that most recruiters look up everything?"

—Recruiter for a Fortune 500 company

Facebook

There are two types of Facebook accounts: personal pages and business pages. This means you should not have two personal pages and use one for professional use and the other for friends and family. It is vital to use the appropriate kind of account for the topic at hand. If the account is to keep up with friends and family, create a personal page; for a business, use a business page. You are not beating the system by not following this protocol; in fact, not using the right page could hurt your efforts to reach a wider market. When promoting a brand, splitting resources in half hurts the overall goal (i.e., having two Facebook pages promoting the same brand splits the amount of likes the brand will get). Unfortunately, most people don't have the attention span to "like" the same thing twice. Focus your efforts on *one* page and start stockpiling fans.

———————————— On the Side ————————————

"I couldn't believe it when one of my clients wrote how much she hated work that week and was ready for Friday. The real issue was that all of her colleagues were reading the same thing. What was she thinking? People who make those mistakes are lucky to have a job. I would never promote someone who wrote that."

—Manager at an IT outsourcing company

Best Practices

- Use appropriate privacy settings, but don't be too trusting. Somebody (employer, family, even law enforcement) seeking to find information about you can always succeed, even with a strict privacy setting.
- Where there is a will, there is a way to find someone on the Internet. Be cautious.
- It's best to develop a custom privacy setting for both your personal and business pages as both of your pages are different in nature and content; therefore, they deserve different attention and management.
- Privacy settings are no longer simply restricted to photos, messages, and friend requests. Facebook has innovated to the level of specifying between friends, acquaintances, family, and others. This allows for the appropriate content to be published to the appropriate audiences and hides the content from others and those who need not view those posts.

- Do not post anything negative about work. Be aware that many employers *do* track Internet usage on company computers.
- Be sensitive to the amount of posts you write. People do not like having their feeds clogged with unnecessary information. This will compel others to unfriend or unlike your account and can ruin a professional or personal relationship.
- Three Facebook posts a day is a good amount for a personal account, unless you have developed into an industry thought leader, in which case make sure to accommodate Facebook posting supply and demand.

YouTube

With billions and billions in traffic, YouTube has become one of the Internet's top sources for visual knowledge. Many brands, companies, products, and services are viewed on YouTube daily, creating newfound revenue. If you're a DIY (do it yourself) or how-to person, YouTube will be a must. YouTube value plays a vital roll in your overall Internet presence and is a stepping-stone that must be in place.

Best Practices

- Before you jump in and make videos, make sure you understand the terms of service.
- Keep up with comments on your videos.
- Use this platform as another way to make new relationships.
- Your YouTube channel design adds legitimacy and therefore should be planned out before you upload the first video.

- Making sure your video formatting is in spec with YouTube requirements will result in more views and quicker growth.

Twitter

Twitter differs than other platforms in terms of content; it's more about *what* is said instead of *who* said it. Searches are more keyword based whereas searches on Facebook focus more on people. If your Twitter handle is used under a pseudonym and content doesn't identify back to you, feel free to be silly and have fun. If your Twitter represents you personally or professionally, filter your thoughts. Twitter gives people a powerful voice and that needs not to be abused. Everything you write on Twitter is public; be careful that you are communicating your brand.

Best Practices

- Be witty and expressive, but be aware that being heard can lead to problems if not executed properly.
- Be mindful that despite the ability to delete a post, people still could have seen it in the brief time it was published. Certain programs allow others to see posts even if deleted, especially if they include profanity.
- Use Twitter as a tool to express insight in your industry.
- Being active in the online community of your interest gives the ability to become a thought leader. Insightful comments provide a basis for industry credibility and mass exposure as a public figure or in reflecting your business.
- Follow those who interest you; this will broaden your horizons, which ultimately leads to new followers.

Followers equal power and leverage.

- If the goal is raising awareness, every follower represents a vast new network of potential viewers, which emphasizes the viral nature of Twitter and social media as a whole.
- Utilize the search box with subjects of interest and find new conversations to join and others to follow.
- Consider following people suggested by Twitter, and take note in trending topics.
- Use a business Twitter account to create business relationships.
- Teach your clients how to follow you and then make sure you keep your tweets professional.
- Be conversational. Use Twitter as a discussion forum; it enables your clients to see that others respect you too.
- Thank people when they make comments.
- Do not be an over-poster; this will make you lose followers. It is important to understand that Twitter allows 140 characters for a reason. People on Twitter are looking for and expecting the bottom line.

Blogging

Anything you blog regarding work can be used against you. Use your professional voice rather than slang. Edit your posts and make sure there are no typos or grammatical errors. Be clear and concise. Don't be too personal, be personable. Keep your opinions to yourself. Make your blog interesting, informative, and useful for readers so they will continue to come back.

———————————— On the Side ————————————

"I can't believe how employees of this company put inappropriate comments online. Do they not realize that what they post affects how I see them based on the choices they make outside of work? They should keep it private; I really don't want to know what they do."

—VP of human resources, national skin care company

Best Practices

- Do not post anything negative about work where colleagues or customers can read it. Manage your settings well and make your information private.
- Be aware that many employers can track Internet usage on company computers.
- The wrong message can drive people away from your brand.

Ask Yourself These Crucial Questions

- Have I figured out the ROI on building my online presence?
- Am I committed to spending at least one hour a week to build my online brand?
- Am I reaching the people I need to reach? If not, what am I doing about it? How do I change that?

Big Mistake

9

Lack of Awareness of Communication Stallers and Stoppers

"The negotiations were going great until
Kruger decided to 'Go Negative'."

"What is necessary to change a person is to change his awareness of himself."
—Abraham Maslow

Have you ever heard of stallers and stoppers in business? Stallers and stoppers are characteristics or behaviors that one exhibits that can stall his or her career or stop it. Over the last twenty years we have trained and worked with more than twenty thousand people. In many of our sessions we ask participants what behaviors make them cringe and "shut down" to the point where they do not want to work with the other person. This chapter focuses on the top answers we repeatedly hear.

Interrupting

"If a is success in life, then a equals x plus y plus z. Work is x; y is play; and z is keeping your mouth shut."
—Albert Einstein

When we ask people what behavior drives them crazy, interrupting is one of the most common answers. Interrupting can halt all communication. It makes other people think that you do not care about what they are saying. In turn, when a person interrupts they have the ability to halt opportunities and the chance to build relationships. There is nothing worse than trying to say something and someone else either finishes your sentence or interrupts you with something they think is more important.

On the Side

"One of my best sales associates asked me for a raise. He does a tremendous job, but he always interrupts when I am speaking. Or worse yet, he finishes my sentences. When I sat down to tell him that he deserved the raise because he had exceeded his goals, he interrupted me and said that he was disappointed that I couldn't give him a raise, but he understood. If he had just let me finish, I think he would have liked my outcome a lot more than his."

—Sales manager at a home improvement store

Best Practices

- Never assume you know what someone is going to tell you.
- Approach every conversation with the thought that you are going to learn something new.
- Focus on what the person is saying, not on what you are going to say next.
- If you like to give advice, stop thinking about your advice and make sure that the person wants advice and isn't just venting.
- When the person stops talking, wait three seconds to make sure they really are finished.

- Many times a customer is telling you exactly how they want to be sold to, and if you are listening you will know how to close the deal.
- Don't interrupt other people in meetings; it's a bad reflection on you.

On the Side

"I have a terrible habit of interrupting. I was with one of my colleagues, and while we were walking to a meeting she was telling me a story. I thought that I knew how she was feeling and what she was about to say. Every time she couldn't think of the word she was trying to capture, I finished her sentence. Finally she said to me, 'Do you think you could just let me finish a thought and tell you how I feel?' I was taken aback to say the least, but after thinking about it, I realized how rude I had been. I now make a very conscious effort not to finish sentences or interrupt."

—Pharmaceutical sales representative

Ask Yourself These Crucial Questions
- How do I feel when someone interrupts me?
- When someone else is speaking, am I listening or am I anxiously waiting to start speaking?
- Do I wait until someone has finished speaking before I join the conversation?

Talking Too Much

"The less said, the better."
—Jane Austen

Good conversation should never be misinterpreted as good communication. When someone asks a direct question, generally they are looking for a concise and direct answer. In the business arena, it is important to stay focused on the business at hand and not be overly communicative about issues that have no bearing. Even in social settings, when people talk too much, other people cannot get out of the conversation quickly enough.

On the Side

"I interviewed an extremely sharp young man for a sales position. He held himself well, his body language was positive—we were off to a good start. I asked him to tell me what he was looking for in a career. When I looked down at my watch, it was thirty minutes later and he was still going. There was no stopping in sight, similar to the Energizer Bunny. No matter what position we're in, it is so important to know when we've oversold. Knowing how to be concise, yet informative, is crucial to communication success."

—VP of sales for an automotive group

Best Practices

- Always be interested, not interesting.
- If the other person keeps looking away, you are probably not holding their attention.
- When you start to notice glazed-over eyes with no reaction to what you are saying, *stop* talking.
- If the other person has not said anything for at least five minutes, they might be thinking about other things.
- Focus on the other person's body language. If they are not looking at you, nodding, or leaning forward, you have lost them.
- Keep personal conversations to a minimum unless in an appropriate environment.
- Keep personal information to a minimum.

Ask Yourself These Crucial Questions

- Has the other person said anything in the last five minutes?
- Am I being as interested as I am interesting?
- How do I get back on track when I realize I have gone off on a tangent that is of no interest to the other person?

Being a Know-It-All

> "People don't care how much you know until they
> know how much you care."
> —Theodore Roosevelt

There is a difference between knowing a lot and being a "know-it-all." How do you know if you're a know-it-all? Have people ever referred to you as a "smart aleck"? If you know everything about everything at all times—or so you think—you may be one of these people. Remember the Johari Window? It's time to get feedback from someone you trust. Being so smart all the time is actually holding you back. No one wants to be with a know-it-all; it's draining, and most of us stop listening. You can't reach your communication goal if people are not hearing what you have to say.

Best Practices
- Remember that there is a time and a place to share what you know.
- Be a listener.
- Ask yourself if people are asking you to contribute to the conversation.
- Ask questions.
- Find a mentor who can help you learn to listen and practice empathy.
- Stop letting your ego get in the way.

Ask Yourself These Crucial Questions

- Do my friends and family joke that I am a know-it-all?
- Do I find myself taking up more than 80 percent of most conversations? How can I make that no more than 50 percent?
- When do I have the opportunity to practice changing my behavior?

Not Being Focused or Paying Full Attention

"I think the one lesson I have learned is that there is no substitute for paying attention."

—Diane Sawyer

No one wants to be discounted. When we do not focus on the other person, we are not only discounting them, we are also making a very crucial communication mistake. When we don't focus on the conversation at hand, we destroy trust. When we are fully present when communicating, we build trust. It starts at a handshake. When shaking someone's hand and using direct eye contact, you build immediate rapport. On the flip side, when you are distracted and looking around, the other person feels discounted. Staying focused is a communication and rapport-building skill that can build long-term relationships.

─────────── On the Side ───────────

"We conducted a management survey, and the participants were going around the room talking about what they

69

respected most about their own managers. One up-and-coming manager said that the one thing that she respected most about her manager was that every time she walked into her office, no matter what her manager was doing, her manager stopped and focused on her. It made her feel important and of value to the team. It also was teaching her how to be a better leader."

—Hospital supervisor

Best Practices

Telephone/Cell Phone

- Stand up, turn away from your desk, and focus on the conversation.
- If it is necessary to take notes, do not start doodling; stay focused.
- Do not start working on other things; the person on the other end will be able to tell.
- Stay engaged or end the conversation before you end a good business relationship.

Meetings

- Put down everything and focus.
- Have a pen in your hand only if you are taking notes on the current conversation.
- Do not use your phone; put it on "do not disturb" or silent.
- Close the door if necessary and do not allow any interruptions.
- Go into a private conference room if necessary.
- Make eye contact.

- Do not have side conversations.
- Keep your body language engaged; do not start fidgeting.
- Stay focused on the conversation or agenda.
- The more respect you give the other person, the more respect you will receive.

───────────────── On the Side ─────────────────

"I am so busy all of the time. When people come to me with their issues, I have a hard time concentrating on what they need me to do because I have a number of to-dos on my own list. I realized that I was forgetting things, not focusing on my employees, and losing the respect of my colleagues. I started carrying around a small notebook and now anytime anyone asks me to do something, I write it down. My coworkers know that I am paying attention to them and listening. It also ensures that I do what I say I'll do without having to keep everything in my memory."

—National accounts manager, luxury goods

Networking

- When shaking hands, make direct eye contact.
- Listen and focus on names so that you can use them and introduce others if necessary.
- Do not look over someone's shoulder to see who else is there.
- Follow through on what you promise; this will let others know that you are reliable and were listening to them.

Ask Yourself These Crucial Questions

- When I am trying to get someone's attention and they do not stop what they are doing, how does that make me feel?
- When someone is talking to me, do I stop everything else I am doing to focus on him or her? If not, what effect do I think that has on our relationship?
- What are some things I can do that will make every person I am speaking to feel valued?

Being Defensive

"When angry, count to ten before you speak; if very angry, a hundred."
—Thomas Jefferson

Have you ever felt your blood pressure rise when someone said or did something to annoy you? Or when someone confronted you about something you did? Defensive behavior usually surfaces in situations where conflict, pressure, or threats are present. Usually a red flag goes up in our minds when we feel attacked, manipulated, judged, or reprimanded.

Generally our ability to think clearly and be rational is compromised while in a defensive behavior mode. It is so easy to react. The hard part is thinking about how your reaction can affect your credibility.

Take the high road always, even when someone puts you on the defensive. This behavior will command respect. Remember that many times their intention is to tell you how they are feeling. If you are on your A-game, you will ask yourself, "What can I learn from what they are telling me? How can I grow from this?" We make mistakes when we think we can't grow from a situation and are more concerned about our ego than the real message.

─────────── On the Side ───────────

"I ran a meeting last week and my colleague came up to me and said, 'I have a great opportunity for you.' I immediately was excited. Then she said, 'When you are running meetings, I want you to be aware of the number of times you say "um" you use and how you repeat sentences when you're not sure what to say.' Well, that was not the opportunity I expected. I immediately began to make excuses. Being self-aware, I then realized that she supports me 100 percent and was only telling me this to grow."

—Financial advisor

Best Practices

- Become more self-aware.
- Know what your hot buttons are.
- Try not to react or be overwhelmed; breathe.
- Realize that you can walk away, think about what has just been said, and deal with it later when you are more rational.
- Stop and say, "I hear what you are saying." This allows the other person to feel heard.
- Use clarifying statements such as, "Let me see if I

understand you correctly . . ." or "I want to make sure I am hearing what you're saying . . . "
- Don't keep talking and telling; ask questions to gain clarity.
- Let your ego go; it's all right not to have the last word.
- React in a way that commands respect and credibility.

Ask Yourself These Crucial Questions
- How do I react when I hear things I disagree with or have a different opinion than someone else?
- What do I do when I read someone else's defensive behavior?
- How can I communicate while I am feeling defensive?

Words That Detract

Have you have ever been in a situation where someone used inappropriate words, dialect, examples, or stories and you just wanted to cringe? Unfortunately these things can stick with us and may affect how we perceive working with that person.

We have all done this. Sometimes we don't even realize what we are doing or saying. Based on the listener's experiences and education, our words can speak volumes.

Some terms have actually become acceptable words because of high usage. The bottom line is that people who know the appropriate usage know when a word is being misused, and it can affect their perceptions.

The following table provides some examples of words or pronunciations that are incorrect, as well as more appropriate words to use instead.

One Step Back	One Step Ahead
Yous guys	All of you
Yeah	Yes
No problem	Of course
Overused words: • OK • Really • You know	Suggestions: • Pause • Listen • Nod
Vulgarity and curse words	Eliminate all vulgarity and curse words from your vocabulary.
I'm doing good	I'm doing well
Gonna	Going to
Wanna	Want to
Irregardless	Regardless
Etiqwett	Etiquette
Gimme	Give me
Totally	Absolutely
Aks	Ask

──────────────── On the Side ────────────────

"Have you ever heard yourself using a certain word and immediately felt like it made you seem less professional or uneducated? I had to cringe during a meeting when I responded to a VP with the word 'totally' and they asked me if I was a Valley Girl. Another time I used the word 'OK' repeatedly and someone commented on how annoying it was to hear the word over and over again. A few other times

I have felt uncomfortable when I say things like 'expecially' instead of 'especially' or 'error on the side of caution' instead of 'err on the side of caution.' I realized how important it is to use proper grammar and avoid slang and casual words because I could see how people perceived me."

—Insurance company project manager

Best Practices

- Ask a mentor or a friend what words they notice you use a lot.
- If people say things like, "That's your word," take a hint.
- Record yourself when doing a presentation or leading a meeting.
- Pause; become comfortable with quiet gaps.
- Use nonverbal gestures.
- Read more and become acquainted with new words.
- When you don't understand the meaning of a word, look it up.
- Ask yourself if certain pronunciations you grew up with are holding you back in your professional life.

Ask Yourself These Crucial Questions

- What are my comfort words when I am filling gaps of quiet space?
- What words do I overuse? If I don't know, who can I ask?
- How do I eliminate these words?

Filler Words When Presenting

Have you ever attended a presentation where you knew the presenter and were astounded by how a seemingly articulate person cracked under pressure? The colleague who speaks clearly and is respected by his team members stammers and stutters. He interjects "um" and "uh" in every other sentence. Why does this happen?

There are many "filler" words in English for when we don't know how to continue in a sentence, such as "hmmm," "er,"and "like."

In general, when speakers say these filler words or perform filler actions (such as licking their lips), they do so unconsciously. They make these sounds or do these actions at a transition point when they are getting ready to move on to another topic or offer an example. The simple act of switching from one topic to another demands a transition, and when one has not been determined by the speaker beforehand, the unconscious fills in. For some, it is a less-than-articulate "uh"; for others it is scratching the head. In either case, the behavior can be stopped.

The best way to eliminate filler words and actions is to substitute one behavior for another. So at points of transition or whenever you feel the need to inject filler, simply *pause*. Take a deep breath and gather your thoughts. The pause that seems so long to you is actually a welcome respite for your audience. They, too, need a break in order to concentrate.

Ask Yourself These Crucial Questions

- What slang or filler words do I use over and over again?
- When other people speak, what do I notice?
- What can I do to eliminate fillers and casual words from my professional life?

Big Mistake

10

Not Turning Roadblocks into Opportunities

"We are all faced with a series of great opportunities
brilliantly disguised as impossible situations."
—Charles R. Swindoll

Many things can get in our way when it comes to communication. We can let them bog us down or we can deal with them to improve our situation and our relationships. The bottom line is that poor business communication can prevent career growth.

Assumptions

In his book *Overcoming Organizational Defenses*, Chris Argyris discusses the Ladder of Inference, a model that explains our thinking process. We all have experiences in our head, and when we process events that happen, we go through a series of steps to reach a conclusion based on what we have already experienced and then we act accordingly.

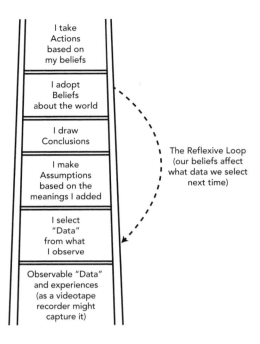

Reprinted from Peter Senge, *The Fifth Discipline Fieldbook.*

In other words, we have information coming in and, based on our observations, we select what we think is appropriate for the situation, we analyze it, and we take action.

Here's the problem. All of this happens very quickly, and what seems to be clear in our own minds is obvious only to us. We select what catches our attention and we dismiss what we don't want to see. We add meaning to what we do see; hence we make assumptions and draw conclusions based on those assumptions.

All of this is happening when we're communicating. In simple terms, we all bring our own set of past experiences and baggage to every interaction. We draw conclusions as to why someone is acting in a certain way and we naturally assume that their motivations, behaviors, wants, desires, likes, and dislikes should match our own. Then our emotions kick in and we start reacting, either positively or negatively. In a work situation, this is where we respond based on our conclusions, and it is often emotional rather than rational.

This happens all day long.

Best Practices

- Be aware of how your assumptions can affect your communication.
- Try to understand the root of your feelings.
- Try to be transparent and let the other person know where you are coming from based on your assumptions, interpretations, and conclusions without being defensive.
- Allow others to test your assumptions without being condescending.
- Use open-ended and nonjudgmental questions rather than questions that exhibit a bias.
- Don't agree or disagree too soon.
- Be respectful.

--- On the Side ---

"I had an employee who was generally a great employee. For the last two months he had not been thorough while documenting his work. When I looked for a piece of client information that should have been documented, it wasn't there. *Of course,* I thought. *He never documents.* My immediate assumptions included: he's lazy, he doesn't follow through, he doesn't do what I ask, he may not be right for the job, he expects a lot but doesn't do his part. . . .

"Based on the interpreted facts and my assumptions, my conclusions were that I had lost respect for this employee. My belief is that what you put into work you get out. My actions, based on my beliefs, were that I needed to reprimand my employee. I started to go through the Ladder of Inference in my mind.

"Initally I did not think about what could be going on with this employee, such as:

- The employee has been struggling at work and was embarrassed to ask for help.
- The documentation is there, but it was in the wrong place.
- I made an error in looking it up.
- He is overwhelmed and can't keep up.
- There is a system glitch and he didn't realize it.
- He is not the right person for the job.

"Due to my awareness that I might be perceiving this incorrectly, I thought about handling the conversation very differently.

"There were possible solutions:

- 'Can you help me understand why the documentation is missing?'
- 'I know that this isn't typical for you, but for the last two months I haven't seen any documentation. Can you tell me what's going on? Help me understand.'

"It is important to start with the awareness that this is taking place. Then we have to change behavior to not make mistakes that can cost us a relationship."

—Director at a hotel group

Ask Yourself These Crucial Questions

- Past experiences are good predictors. Reflecting on past opportunities, what could I do differently in the future?
- Am I looking at all of my solutions?
- What attitude am I choosing when confronted with roadblocks?

Big Mistake

11

Not Focusing on the Details

"Beware of the person who can't
be bothered by details."

—William Feather

As we said at the beginning of this book, we communicate through our actions. These actions communicate our brand and what people can expect from us. The details matter. Dotting your i's and crossing your t's does make a difference. Why is it that we focus on a spot on someone's shirt rather than on what they are saying? Why is it that when someone gives us a limp handshake, we focus on that and not on the skills they bring to the table? If someone misspells our name, we start checking for other mistakes.

─────────── **On the Side** ───────────

"Recently I was planning a large client event and we had chosen a specific caterer. I couldn't believe it when the proposal came and our company name was misspelled. When

I said something, the person didn't apologize but told me they were so busy and that's why it was misspelled. I didn't want to hear an excuse, just an apology."

—Events director for a hedge fund

This book is all about communication details. Here are a few other details that can set you apart and speak loudly even though no words are used.

Best Practices
Tracking and Following Up
- Keep track of conversations and keep your notes in one location.
- Follow up when you say you will.
- Follow up even if you don't know the final status.
- Set reminders.
- If you don't have a good tracking system, find one.
- Be meticulous about keeping everything together.

Handwritten Notes
- Make sure your note has no mistakes, including no crossed-out words.
- A handwritten note should be exactly that, not an e-mail.
- Use a pen.
- Send a note preferably within three days of the event; if you forget and it's late, write it anyway and start with, "I am sorry that it has taken me so long to thank you . . ."

Write Them When:

- You meet a new person.
- A client gives you new business.
- Someone helps you do, get, or accomplish something.
- There is an occasion or congratulations are in order, such as a promotion.
- You want to be at the top of someone's mind or just to say hello.

─────────── On the Side ───────────

"It was not a coincidence when I wrote a note to a client just to say hi and two days later she called to discuss a project for which they wanted to hire us."

—Designer with an architecture firm

Ask Yourself These Crucial Questions

- Have I taken the time to thank the people I work with on a regular basis?
- How will I ensure that I check the details of my work?
- Do I follow up when I say I will? How do I stay on top of my schedule and my to-dos?

Big Mistake

12

Not Giving Precise Feedback

"My apologies if I was too harsh with you."

"Feedback is the breakfast of champions."

—Ken Blanchard

Feedback is communication to a person or a team. Feedback offers both the sender and the receiver an opportunity to grow. Providing feedback is incredibly important and should happen on a regular basis. Feedback can be hard to deliver and receive and can produce conflict if not planned well or if the receiver is close-minded. Yet it is vital to improving performance and building good relationships.

The most important thing about feedback is that just giving feedback is not enough. The information provided needs to be specific, with detailed behavior modification examples. Many people don't know how to change their behavior based on feedback. Thus we need to give people the "how-tos" so that they can modify their behavior.

Best Practices

- Feedback must be specific and focused on an observable behavior: "I noticed when you checked in Mr. Smith . . ." versus "When you check people in . . ."
- Be timely but not reactive.

- Feedback must be measurable and achievable. Do not say things like, "I feel like you can try harder." Rather, "When checking in clients, smile and make eye contact."
- Ask the recipient of the feedback for their ownership of the issue and their commitment to improvement.
- Make sure you let the person know you support them, just not the behavior.
- Criticize the behavior, not the person.

Feedback Conversation Planning

The following questions will help you prepare when you need to provide feedback to others.

- What is the communication style of the person receiving the feedback?
- What is going to make this person take notice of what you are saying?
- What are *three* points you want to make? If you cover too many points, you will lose focus.
- What are the benefits to the person if they change the behavior? That is, what's in it for them?
- What are the risks to both the person and the company if they don't change the behavior at hand?
- What questions do you anticipate them asking as you give feedback?
- What solutions and timeline can you both come up with during the feedback session?
- How will you measure behavioral changes?

——————————— On the Side ———————————

"I was sitting in a meeting and my boss completely undermined what I said in front of everyone. She also neglected to mention that I had done the work she presented and gave herself full credit. She asked for feedback after the meeting. I was commited to making her feel comfortable yet let her know that her actions affect the team. I was clear and concise and focused on specific actions, not her as a person. I said, 'During the meeting I did not receive credit for all of the work I had done. When I made a comment, I felt as though you undermined me when you said that you wouldn't handle the situation that way. My goal is to deliver the best results for this team and a unified relationship. What is your goal?'

"Fortunately my boss received the feedback well and we have a much stronger working relationship."

—Customer service agent for a home design firm

Ask Yourself These Crucial Questions

- What have I learned from feedback others have given me?
- How will I plan out my next feedback session?
- How will I receive feedback going forward? What can I learn from this?

Big Mistake

13

Not Adapting to Different Communication Styles

"Why must we always communicate? Why can't
you just listen to me?"

"Insanity: doing the same thing over and over again
and expecting different results."
—Albert Einstein

In today's corporate environment, we are missing an opportunity to better connect when we do not recognize and adapt to different communication styles. We allow ourselves to get frustrated with how other people handle situations, timelines, and conversations. To be most effective, we must realize that people work at different speeds and in different ways.

Let's explore the normal behaviors that we see on a day-to-day basis. We all have natural communication tendencies that can change based on the situation and the environment. Wouldn't you agree that some people dominate a conversation and some sit back and listen? Some want all the details while others are thinking about who is going to be involved. Some want to control the project and others want to take a backseat because they don't know enough. Some people are like chameleons and you're not sure what their position is.

There are many assessment tools available that analyze personality styles and provide insight into who we are and how we handle everyday situations and dealings with other people. The key is our own awareness and what we do with the information to improve and make the most of our communications.

The following are brief examples for you to think about regarding knowing yourself, reading others, and adapting. Keep in mind that you will likely see a little of yourself in all of these people, and you will also relate to one or two more closely.

Let's talk about Joe. Joe is a get-it-done kind of guy. He says it like it is, he always wants the bottom line, and he doesn't like small talk unless he's the one making it. He focuses on accomplishing tasks as quickly as possible. He seems to procrastinate because he's got a lot on his plate, and he thrives on the challenge of getting his work done in the nick of time. His desk is messy while he's juggling multiple tasks. When asked, he knows where things are, or at least he makes others think he knows. Joe is direct and doesn't avoid confrontation. At times it seems as though he doesn't care about others' feelings because he's so focused on the task rather than the person. Some people would even say that Joe thinks it's all about him. He's really confident and can be intimidating at times. Joe has to be in control. Sometimes it's fun working with him because of his energy. He loves taking risks. Joe is an asset to the team because he is a visionary who gets things done.

How do you deal with Joe? Here are some best practices:
- Stay focused on the bottom line.
- Get to the point quickly.
- Don't give him all of the details unless he asks, and even then be brief.
- Always give him an executive summary with the support information behind it.
- Openly admire how well he did on a project.

- Tell him when you need his help and time rather than asking when he has the time. He never has the time—he's busy.
- Listen when he's talking and nod to show you're listening.

Sally works with Joe. Sally is a real people person who is very enthusiastic and energetic. She loves to know what's going on with everyone and everything and likes to feel included. Sally gets to work early to ensure that she is seen and has time to chat with her friends. She is impulsive, taking on any new project she's asked to be a part of. Yet finishing them is a different story because she has too much going on. She loves generating ideas and looks at the people and fun factor of any project. Routine tasks seem tedious and mundane. Sally is the first to say hello in the morning and greets everyone she walks by during the day. She will call or e-mail multiple times because when she has a question she wants to know the answer to right away. Unfortunately, she tends to leave her notes at home. Sally sometimes gets in trouble because she likes to gossip since she knows so much about so many. Yet when someone gets angry with her, she gets incredibly upset because she wants everyone to like her. Sally is an asset to the team because of her people skills.

How do you deal with Sally? Here are some best practices:
- Keep Sally in the loop and include her in meetings.
- Ask for her ideas.
- Allow her to provide input.
- Show interest in her work.
- Don't just send her e-mails; invest in face time or time on the phone.
- Allow her to work on new projects.

Jeff is the peacekeeper of the bunch. He doesn't like to rock the boat at all, although he will if it is necessary. Jeff is concerned about how things affect the team. He likes to make thoughtful decisions and carefully examine all of the ramifications of his decision. Jeff likes to take time to process his thoughts. Everyone in the office knows that they can go to Jeff when they need someone to listen. He always has the patience to hear them and does not need to add his two cents. Jeff is very accommodating most of the time. He does seem to get upset when he has too much on his plate and doesn't feel that he can finish the job in the specified amount of time and as well as he would like. Jeff is methodical and consistent.

How do you deal with Jeff? Here are some best practices:
- Show respect for his caution in making decisions.
- Make decisions with him collaboratively.
- Have mutually agreed-upon deadlines.
- Show a genuine interest in his personal life.
- Understand his need for team input.
- Show sincere appreciation when he does something for you.

Cheryl is in the accounting department. She is all about facts, quality, accuracy, and details. Cheryl doesn't have a lot of time to discuss personal issues with her coworkers. Her privacy is important to her. When she arrives in the morning, she gets to work immediately and doesn't have the time or the interest to engage in chitchat. Cheryl works hard to make sure that her work is of the highest quality, so when she gets criticized or critiqued, she is not happy. However, she is quick to criticize others when she feels that someone is not doing their job well.

When given a report that lacks sufficient detail, Cheryl feels that it is a waste of her time to read it. She consistently asks her coworkers to fill in the detail so that her analysis can be more thorough. Cheryl is task-oriented and very diplomatic. She really doesn't enjoy working with people who are outwardly passionate or enthusiastic. She would prefer the facts in a concise manner.

How do you deal with Cheryl? Here are some best practices:
- Focus on the facts.
- Don't get into your personal issues unless you have a strong personal relationship.
- Let her take time to process a decision; don't expect an immediate resolution.
- Be specific when being critical and realize she won't like what you say because it affects her drive for perfection.
- Be prepared to give the details that back up any overview or summary.
- Offer opportunities that let her use her expertise.

Best Practices
- Know whether someone is a talker or a listener, and adapt accordingly.
  - » If they are a talker, let them talk.
  - » If they are a listener, ask questions to bring them out.
- Be aware if you are talking too much.
- Know whether someone is task-oriented or people-oriented, and try to adapt.
- If the other person likes to talk about personal matters, be interested in their lives and then move on to the business at hand.

- Realize that most people are not trying to annoy others but are doing what comes naturally to them.

Joe, Sally, Jeff, and Cheryl were driving to a meeting three hours away. Obviously Joe was the driver and Sally was the copilot. Cheryl kept looking over Joe's shoulder, upset that he seemed to be going faster than the speed limit. Joe was annoyed that Cheryl kept making comments. Jeff was a little hungry and pulled out his baggie of labeled carrots and offered some to the group. He had brought enough for everyone. Sally had M&M's and chips. Cheryl had packed a cooler—everything in its place—full of water and sandwiches. Joe was running late so he had no snacks.

As Cheryl ate her sandwich, she looked at Sally and again commented on Joe's speed. Sally just looked at her and smiled; there was no way she was saying anything to Joe. Joe overheard and said to the others, "Stop worrying about my speed! Bottom line, let me do the driving!"

And off they went.

Ask Yourself These Crucial Questions

- Do I adapt to other people or do I do what is natural to my communication style?
- Do I notice how sometimes I have rapport with others and sometimes building rapport is difficult?
- Can I identify the preferred communication style of everyone I work with and start to adapt to his or her preferred style?

Big Mistake

14

Not Reacting Professionally

"My behavior is my reaction; my reaction is my behavior"

—Unknown

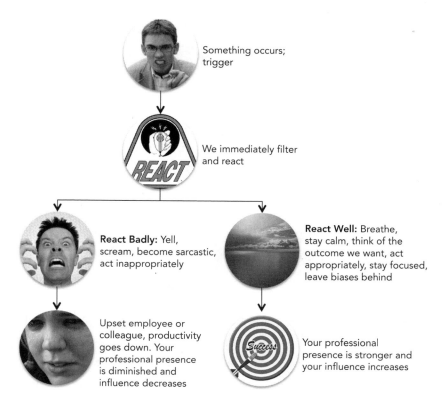

Something occurs; trigger

We immediately filter and react

React Badly: Yell, scream, become sarcastic, act inappropriately

React Well: Breathe, stay calm, think of the outcome we want, act appropriately, stay focused, leave biases behind

Upset employee or colleague, productivity goes down. Your professional presence is diminished and influence decreases

Your professional presence is stronger and your influence increases

Have you ever reacted to a situation and afterward wished you had handled it differently? You know that you keep repeating a similar reaction and getting the same feeling of annoyance, hurt, frustration, or disdain. You want to change your reaction, but you're just not sure how to do so. You know that this is hurting your communication and effectiveness with others. We call this "going down the rat hole."

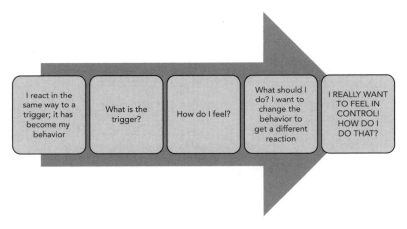

Stop and think about what is going on in your mind. We react to others because we have a preconceived idea of what they want based on previous experience and assumptions.

Something happens that triggers a reaction from you and leaves you thinking, "If only I hadn't . . . if only I had handled it differently . . . now I feel so angry, frustrated, and cornered."

Why do we continue to react in the same way knowing that we'll regret our actions later? One cannot stop events that trigger reactions. We can, however, become aware of what is happening and look at our own behavior and reactions. All of us walk around with preconceived ideas or stories in our heads of how "things" should be, how others expect us to be, and what we think we need to show people.

─────────────── On the Side ───────────────

"Bob felt that every time he had to present at an executive meeting he needed to show how clever he was and how much he had researched the issue. This was the trigger that caused him to go on and on and never get to the point. Unfortunately the executives in his company started to feel that he did not understand the big picture, when, in reality, Bob thought that all the facts he was giving were showing how much he understood. When Bob recognized this trigger and realized that he did not have to prove how clever he was, he changed his delivery to the executive team. Bob let go of the 'story' in his head. The executive team at his company now recognizes him as one of the most competent individuals who always 'hits the target.'"

—Harriet Whiting, vice president at Image Dynamics

Best Practices

- When you find yourself going down the "rat hole" and not getting results, *stop*.
- Write down your triggers, those things that happen around you that cause you to react negatively.
- Memorize those triggers and become aware of them immediately.
- As soon as you are triggered, stop and think about your reaction.
- Do not assume what other people are thinking; that is a trigger that hurts our behaviors.
- Realize that the "story" in your head may not be reality.
- Start noticing how your reactions may trigger others and figure out how to change those reactions.

- If you do not know how to change your behavior, you may want to look into working with an executive coach.

Ask Yourself These Crucial Questions

- Have I ever stopped when I find myself reacting negatively and become aware of *how* I am feeling and behaving?
- What is triggering my reaction and what can I do to change my reaction?
- What do I need to ask to gain more clarity to change my behavior?

Big Mistake

15

Bloopers and Blunders:
What We Notice When
We're Out and About

"Experience is simply the name
we give our mistakes."
—Oscar Wilde

This chapter is like the outtakes at the end of a movie. It encompasses all of those things we do that could get us into trouble and hurt our reputations without us realizing it.

Driving

Be careful that you don't cut off people or use improper body language. Who knows—you could end up in a meeting with that person in the next lane. It has happened before and it will happen again.

Waiting in Line

Don't cut in line, and don't say something you'll be sorry for as you stand in line. That person you cut in front of or the person who hears you say something rude could be the person interviewing you for a job, your new colleague, or the new VP in your company. This applies to all situations, from the grocery store to checking in at a security desk at a business.

Traveling

You never know who someone is or where they will turn up. Being on your A-game at all times will only help you.

Networking Events

You're not there to eat. There's nothing worse than speaking with someone who is talking with their mouth filled with food. Stay positive; no one likes to be around a negative person.

Bathroom

Wash your hands. If you don't, someone else in there will definitely come out and tell their friends or colleagues that you didn't.

Airplanes and Airports

Don't be in such a hurry that you become impolite. Everyone on your plane is going to the same place at the same time. You can't pass someone and get to your destination any faster than they can.

Additionally, if you see that someone may need help, such as stowing a bag in the overhead compartment, ask if you can be of assistance.

Restaurants and Stores

Be nice to servers and sales associates. People show their lack of character when they are rude to the person "serving" them. We may think that rudeness is acceptable when we don't get the service we expect, but it reflects badly on the person with the rude behavior.

Big Mistake

16

Not Communicating Value

"A brand is a living entity—and it is enriched or undermined cumulatively over time, the product of a thousand small gestures."
—Michael Eisner

What is value and how does something become valuable? By investing in your brand and the behaviors that support it, you communicate value.

Everything we have put in this book builds your value. Everything and everyone has intrinsic value. You have to communicate your value so that others see you as valuable. Investing in relationships and being aware of best practices for all communication methods and modes builds your value over time.

You build value:

- When you help someone else achieve their goal
- When you invest in someone else's growth
- When you spend time learning about another person, their company, their goals, and their needs and wants
- Over time
- When you pay attention to the details

- By remembering the details someone has taken the time to share
- When you go the extra mile
- When you are consistent
- When you do what you say you are going to do
- When you work hard at both your relationship and the actual work
- When you are responsive in a timely manner
- When you listen
- When you are not always selling yourself or your product but when you are seeking to understand
- When you take the time to pick up the phone or visit someone, not just send an e-mail
- When you send a handwritten note
- When you are not arrogant or a know-it-all
- When you are a learner
- When you think about what you say and how you say it
- When you genuinely care

References

Argyris, Chris. *Overcoming Organizational Defenses: Facilitating Organizational Leadership*. Boston: Allyn and Bacon, 1990.

Luft, Joseph and Harry Ingham. "The Johari window, a graphic model of interpersonal awareness." In *Proceedings of the Western Training Laboratory in Group Development*. Los Angeles: UCLA, 1955.

Mehrabian, Albert and Susan R. Ferris. "Inference of attitudes from nonverbal communication in two channels." *Journal of Consulting Psychology* 31 (1967): 248–252.

Mehrabian, Albert and Morton Wiener. "Decoding of inconsistent communications."*Journal of Personality and Social Psychology* 6 (1967): 109–114.

Senge, Peter M. et al. *The Fifth Discipline Fieldbook: Strategies and Tools for Building a Learning Organization*. New York: Currency, Doubleday, 1994.

About the Authors

Kim Zoller and Kerry Preston are recognized experts in business protocol, executive edge, branding, leadership development, and presentation and communication skills, as well as customer service and sales training. Kim and Kerry work with organizations to develop their people and their processes to be as successful as they can in an ever-changing and competitive marketplace. Together they lead Image Dynamics, the most innovative total-solution training and development company. Both Kim and Kerry are dynamic international speakers who assist individuals and companies with the necessary tools to be successful in today's competitive market. Over the last twenty years they have trained more than twenty thousand individuals.